Macro and Micro Economics Made Easy For Beginners

Roggie Clark

Copyright

Title: Macro and Micro Economics Made Easy For Beginners
Author: Roggie Clark

Disclaimer

The views and opinions expressed in this book are those of the author and do not necessarily reflect the official policy or position of any individual, company, or organization cited or referenced in the text. The author is not affiliated with any of the individuals, companies, or organizations mentioned in the text, nor does the author receive any form of compensation for citing or referencing them.

The professional information in this text is distributed on an "as is" basis, without warranty. While every precaution has been taken in the preparation of the text, neither the author nor the publisher shall have any liability to any person or entity with respect to any loss or damage caused or alleged to be caused directly or indirectly by the instructions contained in this text or by the computer software and hardware products described in it.

The author nor the publisher does not guarantee any specific results or outcomes, and the information provided in this text should not be construed as professional advice. Readers should always consult with a qualified professional before making any significant changes to their website or business.

By reading this text, you agree that the author nor the publisher is responsible for any direct, indirect, incidental, or consequential damages that may arise from the use of the information provided. You assume full responsibility for any actions taken based on the information presented in this text.

College Or University Usage

I recommend that college deans and professors consider this book for their curriculum; as well as a resource for your students to use for their own research. If you are interested in using the book for your course or having your bookstore source it for students to purchase, you can reach out to me directly.

Please email me at **bouncerankseo@gmail.com**. In your email, please include the following information:

- Your name
- The school you represent
- The class size you are teaching
- The length of your course (e.g. 6-week course, 12-week course, etc.)
- Any other important information I should know

My administrative assistant will email you back within 24 - 48 hours with rates, and an information sheet to use for your class.

Table Of Contents

Chapter 1: Introduction

I see that you are diving more into the world of economics, I hope you are eager to make sense of how the world works. You might be curious about why prices rise and fall, why some markets boom while others bust.

Maybe you've even started to wonder how all these theories and graphs you hear the media, businesses and politicians make connects to real-life decisions. Before you get lost in the sauce, take a step back. Economics isn't just about abstract ideas—it's the key to understanding the choices people like you and me make everyday, and the forces shaping our society as a whole. Once you see how it all fits together, you'll be hooked like me.

Welcome to the **Basics of Economics For Beginners Students, Business Owners, and Marketers**, where we uncover the power of economics and how it influences businesses, and policy decision makers. As a beginner, you should constantly be studying consumer behavior, anticipating trends, and examining new policies and how they relate to your life.

This book is designed to show you how a solid understanding of economic concepts can elevate your psyche, helping you make smarter decisions, forecast market shifts, and if you are a marketer, or business owner, be able to create campaigns that align perfectly with customer needs and market realities.

Inside this playbook, you'll find practical ways to navigate market forces that are often overlooked but essential to winning in competitive landscapes. Think of concepts like **Price Elasticity**, which allows you to anticipate customer reactions to price changes, or the **Consumer Price Index (CPI)**, which shows you how inflation and economic shifts are shaping consumer spending.

You'll learn how economic markers like these and others can shape your decision making. With each chapter, you'll gain meaningful insights that take you from reactive to proactive, equipping you to spot trends before they happen and adjust your strategies with confidence and ease.

In the book I provide real-world examples, scenarios, and straightforward explanations, you'll uncover how you can apply concepts like **Supply** and **Demand**, **Utility**, **Consumer Choice Theory** and **Purchasing Power** to your real life. You'll discover why consumers like you and me make the decisions we do—and how to use that knowledge to make better decisions. This book will walk you through the economic landscapes where customers like you and me live, giving you the tools to pivot with the economy, anticipate business decisions, and ultimately get ahead.

Let's dive in and unlock the powerful, practical side of economics that everyone needs to succeed! Okay so now that you have a solid introduction of what to expect from this book, let's get into the basics, and that is **Part I: The Foundations of Economics**:

Chapter 2: Understanding Supply, Demand, and Market Equilibrium

In this chapter, we'll explore the fundamental economic principles of **Supply**, **Demand**, and **Market Equilibrium**. These concepts are cornerstones of economics, shaping consumer behavior and influencing the broader economy. For marketers and business owners, understanding these principles is crucial for making informed decisions about pricing, product availability, and promotional strategies. Let's dive in.

Basics of Supply and Demand

The phrase *"supply and demand"* is one of the most recognizable terms in economics. At its core:

- **Supply** refers to the quantity of a product or service that producers are willing and able to offer at different prices.
- **Demand** represents the amount of a product or service that consumers are willing and able to buy at various price points.

Although the definitions seem simple, the interaction between supply and demand can be complex. Consumer preferences, production costs, external factors (like market trends or global events), and even psychological triggers can influence supply and demand, making it a dynamic relationship.

The Supply Curve and Demand Curve

Economists use **curves** to visualize how supply and demand respond to price changes. These curves provide a snapshot of economic behavior in a given market.

1. **The Supply Curve**
    - The supply curve shows the relationship between the price of a product and the quantity suppliers are willing to produce.

    - Typically, as the price of a product increases, suppliers are more incentivized to produce and sell it. For example, if smartphones fetch a higher price, manufacturers may allocate more resources to produce them, increasing supply. This upward-sloping curve reflects that trend.
2. **The Demand Curve**
    - The demand curve illustrates the relationship between price and the quantity consumers are willing to buy.
    - Generally, as prices decrease, demand increases. For instance, if a coffee chain reduces its prices, more customers are likely to purchase coffee. Conversely, when prices rise, demand tends to decline. This behavior is captured in the downward-sloping demand curve.

It's important to note that these curves are influenced by factors beyond price, such as consumer income, preferences, and the availability of substitutes.

Market Equilibrium and Price Setting

Market Equilibrium occurs when the quantity of a product that consumers want to buy (demand) matches the quantity that producers are willing to sell (supply) at a specific price. This equilibrium price ensures that the market is "balanced," meaning there are no shortages or surpluses of the product.

Here's why this matters for businesses:

- **If the price is too high**, supply exceeds demand, leading to a surplus (unsold products).
- **If the price is too low**, demand exceeds supply, causing shortages (consumers can't get the product).

For marketers and business owners, setting the right price is both an art and a science. Effective pricing strategies involve finding the "sweet spot" where:

- Consumers perceive value in the product and are willing to pay.
- Businesses earn enough profit to sustain operations and invest in growth.

For example, during a holiday season, a toy company may increase supply and adjust pricing based on expected demand surges for specific products. By analyzing trends and anticipating equilibrium, they can avoid overstocking or losing sales.

Beyond the Basics: Consumer Psychology and Market Dynamics

Understanding supply and demand goes beyond economics—it taps into human psychology. Consumer behavior often defies strict logic. Emotional triggers, trends, or even fear of missing out (FOMO) can create unexpected spikes in demand. Likewise, perceived scarcity (a limited-edition product) can influence purchasing decisions, even if the price is higher than usual.

Moreover, external factors like inflation, global supply chain disruptions, or cultural shifts can significantly impact market dynamics. For example, a sudden increase in demand for sustainable products has forced companies to adapt their supply chains and pricing strategies.

Practical Applications for Marketers and Business Owners

By mastering the principles of supply, demand, and market equilibrium, business owners and marketers can:

1. **Predict Consumer Behavior:** Anticipating how consumers will react to price changes or product availability can guide marketing campaigns.
2. **Optimize Pricing Strategies:** Knowing when to adjust prices to align with consumer willingness to pay ensures profitability while maintaining demand.
3. **Balance Supply and Demand:** Avoiding surpluses or shortages minimizes waste and maximizes sales potential.

For instance, if a company knows demand for winter clothing peaks in December, they can increase production in advance while offering promotional pricing during the offseason to balance supply and demand year-round.

Wrap - Up

Understanding the interplay between supply, demand, and market equilibrium equips marketers and business owners with powerful tools to make informed decisions. These concepts provide a framework for balancing pricing, product availability, and consumer interest. But more importantly, they open the door to deeper insights into the psychological and emotional factors

Cross-Elasticity of Demand

Another crucial concept is **Cross-Elasticity of Demand**, which examines how the price of one product affects the demand for another. This relationship is particularly evident in **substitute goods** and **complementary goods**.

1. **Substitute Goods**
   Substitute goods are products that consumers can switch between based on price. For example, if the price of a popular soda brand increases, consumers might opt for a store-brand soda with similar characteristics at a lower cost. This is an example of **positive cross-elasticity**, where demand for one product rises as the price of a substitute increases.
2. **Complementary Goods**
   Complementary goods are products that are often purchased together, such as peanut butter and jelly. If the price of peanut butter drops, demand for jelly might increase because consumers are more likely to pair these items. This reflects **negative cross-elasticity**, where a price decrease in one product leads to increased demand for a related product.

While these examples seem intuitive, real-world dynamics often complicate the theoretical framework. For instance, the shift from gasoline-powered cars to electric vehicles isn't as straightforward as theory might suggest. If the cost of owning a gasoline car rises significantly, demand for electric vehicles should, in theory, increase. However, factors like the high upfront cost of electric cars, limited charging infrastructure, and concerns about battery safety can deter consumers. This illustrates how emotional and practical considerations often override purely economic calculations.

Similarly, businesses can influence cross-elasticity by shaping consumer perceptions. For example, even if store-brand soda is cheaper, consumers may stick with the name-brand option if they perceive it as superior in taste or quality. Likewise, with complementary goods, a price drop in peanut butter might not automatically lead to increased jelly sales; consumers might stockpile peanut butter instead or redirect their savings elsewhere.

Inelastic Demand and Cost-Benefit Analysis

Some products and services appear to have **Inelastic Demand**, meaning consumers continue to purchase them despite price increases. Gasoline is a common example. Many consumers rely on gasoline for essential travel, leaving them with few immediate alternatives. However, even gasoline is not perfectly inelastic. Over time, sustained price hikes can prompt changes in behavior, such as reduced driving, increased carpooling, or a shift toward public transportation.

Here, the concept of **Cost-Benefit Analysis** plays a crucial role. Consumers weigh the importance of their destination or activity against the cost of reaching it. If the benefit of traveling outweighs the cost of gasoline, they'll continue to pay the higher price. However, if prices cross a critical threshold, consumers may adjust their habits.

This underscores an important point: even products that seem inelastic have limits. By analyzing these limits, businesses can anticipate consumer responses to price changes and develop strategies to mitigate demand fluctuations.

Practical Applications for Businesses and Marketers

The concepts of elasticity and cross-elasticity aren't just academic—they're tools for actionable business strategies. Here's how understanding these principles can benefit your business:

- **Pricing Strategies**: Use elasticity data to determine optimal pricing. For elastic goods, competitive pricing can maintain demand, while for inelastic goods, modest price increases can boost revenue without significantly affecting sales.
- **Promotional Campaigns**: Align discounts and offers with consumer sensitivity to price changes. For complementary goods, bundling promotions can drive sales for both products.
- **Product Development**: Create products with features that enhance perceived value, reducing their price elasticity. This can help justify premium pricing even in competitive markets.

Wrap - Up

Understanding elasticity is a powerful way to bridge economic theory and business strategy. By recognizing how price changes influence consumer behavior, businesses can make smarter decisions about pricing, promotions, and product positioning. Whether you're navigating market challenges or planning a new campaign, a clear grasp of elasticity enables you to align your strategies with consumer needs, ensuring long-term success and profitability.

Chapter 4: Utility and Consumer Choice Theory

In this chapter, we will explore **Consumer Choice Theory** and the concept of **Utility** and how understanding these can help you better grasp the decision-making process that consumers use when choosing which products and services to purchase. Let's start with **Utility**.

Utility

Utility is a measure of the satisfaction or pleasure that a person derives from consuming or using a product or service. In essence, it reflects the value that makes someone think, "This is worth buying," or, "This product or service can solve my problems or fulfill my needs."

Utility isn't a fixed value—it changes based on context, preferences, and how much of the product the person has already consumed. To make better decisions, consumers and businesses must evaluate different aspects of utility.

Types of Utility

There are six primary types of utility that describe how products and services deliver satisfaction: **Form Utility**, **Place Utility**, **Time Utility**, **Possession Utility**, **Information Utility**, and **Service Utility**. Additionally, there are two other key types—**Total Utility** and **Marginal Utility**—that explain the levels and changes in satisfaction over time. Let's explore these types of utility in more detail.

Form Utility

Form utility arises from the design, construction, or transformation of a product into something useful or desirable. A product provides form utility when its creation or design fulfills a specific need or want.

Example: A piece of raw wood may have little value to the average person, but when it's used to build a house, it becomes highly valuable. Transforming the wood into something functional adds form utility.

Place Utility

Place utility is created when a product is available where consumers need it most. Even the best product has limited value if it's not in the right location.

Example: A vending machine stocked with snacks and drinks at a busy train station offers high place utility because it provides convenient access to items travelers might need. However, the same machine in a health food store may have little place utility because the products are irrelevant to the audience there.

Time Utility

Time utility is the value derived from a product being available at the right time. Timing is critical in making a product or service more useful or desirable.

Example: Ice cream on a hot summer day has high time utility, just as a snow shovel becomes most valuable during a winter snowstorm. Similarly, a birthday card holds the greatest utility during someone's birthday, and a wedding dress is most useful for a wedding.

Possession Utility

Possession utility refers to the ability of consumers to own and use a product or service. True value is realized when a consumer can take the product home or benefit from it personally.

Example: A bicycle in a store looks exciting, but its actual value is realized when the consumer buys it and rides it. Ownership examples like houses or cars can be more complex, as actual ownership requires fulfillment of financial obligations like mortgage payments or car notes. True possession utility reflects actual ownership rather than perceived ownership.

Information Utility

Information utility is the value derived from knowing about a product or service, its benefits, or how to use it. Without this knowledge, even the best products can seem irrelevant.

Example: A package labeled "100% organic honey" highlights why the product is valuable, making it more attractive to buyers. Similarly, a health supplement is more likely to sell if its benefits are clearly communicated.

Service Utility

Service utility enhances the appeal of a product or service by providing additional options, features, or support that make it easier or more enjoyable to use.

Example: A warranty on a new appliance, free installation for furniture, or a downloadable add-on for a video game all enhance service utility. These extras make the purchase more appealing and the product more enjoyable in the long term.

How These Utilities Work Together

Utilities are not isolated—they work together to explain why products or services are valuable to consumers. Let's use a simple example:

Imagine a child, Alex, at a pizzeria.

1. The pizza offers **form utility** because it is prepared in a way that makes it enjoyable to eat.
2. It has **place utility** because it's conveniently located at the pizzeria where Alex can buy it.
3. The pizza provides **time utility** because Alex is hungry right now, making the meal urgent and desirable.
4. It has **possession utility** because Alex can purchase the pizza and take ownership of it.
5. Finally, it has **information utility** because the menu describes the pizza, helping Alex make an informed choice.

This example demonstrates how utilities interact to create a compelling consumer experience.

Total Utility and Marginal Utility

In addition to the six types of utility, two key concepts—**Total Utility** and **Marginal Utility**—help explain how much satisfaction consumers gain and how it changes over time.

Total Utility (TU)

Total utility is the cumulative satisfaction or happiness derived from consuming a certain quantity of a product or service.

Example: If eating three ice cream cones makes you happy, the total enjoyment you get from all three cones is your total utility. Similarly, a child playing with five toy cars may find joy in all five combined, which represents their total utility.

Marginal Utility (MU)

Marginal utility is the additional satisfaction gained from consuming one more unit of a product or service.

Example: Eating one slice of pizza may make you happy, but eating a second slice increases your happiness further. This increase is the marginal utility of the second slice.

The Law of Diminishing Marginal Utility

The **law of diminishing marginal utility** states that as a person consumes more units of a product or service, the additional satisfaction (marginal utility) from each extra unit tends to decrease.

Examples:

1. You eat the first slice of pizza—it's delicious! The second slice is also enjoyable but not as exciting. By the third slice, you may start feeling full, and by the fourth, you could feel uncomfortable. This diminishing enjoyment illustrates the principle.
2. If a child already owns 10 toy cars, getting one more may not bring much additional happiness. However, the first car they receive could be incredibly exciting.

Total and Marginal Utility in Action

Think of total utility as the overall happiness a product or service provides over time, while marginal utility reflects the added value of each unit consumed.

Revisiting Alex's pizza example:

- If Alex orders an 8-slice pizza, the total enjoyment he gets from the entire pizza is the **total utility**.
- The added enjoyment he feels with each slice represents the **marginal utility**. However, if Alex eats several slices and starts feeling full, the satisfaction from each additional slice will decrease, demonstrating the **law of diminishing marginal utility**.

Understanding total and marginal utility helps businesses and marketers forecast how consumers will perceive the value of their products over time, allowing them to make informed decisions about pricing, production, and promotional strategies.

Consumer Choice Theory

While utility explains satisfaction with a specific offering, Consumer Choice Theory delves into how people make decisions when faced with multiple options. This theory assumes that consumers act rationally, seeking to maximize their utility within the confines of their budget. At its core, Consumer Choice Theory examines how individuals allocate their limited resources (income) to select products or services that provide the most utility – essentially, the best value for their money.

Assumptions of Consumer Choice Theory

Consumer Choice Theory operates on several key assumptions about consumer behavior:

1. **Rational Decision-Making**: Consumers aim to maximize utility and make decisions logically.
2. **Budget Constraints**: Consumers have limited income and must prioritize their choices accordingly.
3. **Price Awareness**: Consumers are aware of the prices of goods and services.
4. **Clear Preferences**: Preferences are complete (consumers can rank their choices) and transitive (if $A > B$ and $B > C$, then $A > C$).

Budget Constraints and Consumer Choices

The budget constraint represents the combinations of goods and services a consumer can afford, given their income and the prices of those goods. Mathematically, this is expressed as:

Px

Where:

- **Px** and **Py** are the prices of goods/services x and y, respectively.
- **Qx** and **Qy** are the quantities of goods/services x and y, respectively.

Consumers typically aim to choose a combination where the total cost of goods/services aligns with or is less than their budget.

Indifference Curves and Marginal Rate of Substitution

An indifference curve is a graphical tool that illustrates combinations of two goods or services that yield the same level of utility to the consumer. Points on the curve represent situations where the consumer is indifferent between the two options. For example, if a consumer enjoys both hot dogs and hamburgers, they might be equally satisfied with a combination of 14 hot dogs and 20 hamburgers, 10 hot dogs and 26 hamburgers, or 9 hot dogs and 41 hamburgers. Each combination provides the same utility.

The slope of an indifference curve, known as the **Marginal Rate of Substitution (MRS)**, indicates the rate at which a consumer is willing to trade one good for another while maintaining the same utility level. The MRS is where the consumer's budget constraint is tangent to the highest possible indifference curve, satisfying:

$$MRS = \frac{Px}{Py}$$

At this point, the rate at which the consumer is willing to trade one good for another matches the rate allowed by the market based on prices. This represents the optimal choice where consumers maximize utility.

Utility Maximization and Demand

Consumer Choice Theory explains the derivation of the demand curve. As the price of a good or service changes, the consumer adjusts their consumption to maximize utility. This behavior leads to shifts in the quantity demanded and provides a foundational understanding of consumer demand.

Critiques of Consumer Choice Theory

Despite its theoretical value, Consumer Choice Theory is not without limitations. Here are some of the main critiques:

1. **Assumption of Rationality**:
    - *Critique*: In reality, consumers often make decisions influenced by emotions, biases, and incomplete information. Impulse buying, brand loyalty, and peer influence can lead to choices that deviate from rational utility maximization. For example, a consumer may buy an expensive handbag not because it provides the highest utility but because it signals status or satisfies emotional desires.
2. **Over-Simplified Preferences**:
    - *Critique*: The theory assumes consistent and clear preferences, which can be unrealistic. Preferences can shift based on context, social trends, or advertising. For instance, a consumer might prefer one type of soda at a party but choose a different brand at a health-focused event.
3. **Ignorance of External Influences**:
    - *Critique*: Consumer behavior is heavily influenced by social, cultural, and environmental factors, which the theory often overlooks. For example, a consumer might purchase an eco-friendly product not solely for personal utility but due to social pressure to appear environmentally conscious.

4. **Limited Role of Information**:
   - *Critique*: The theory presumes consumers have complete and objective information, which is often not the case. In real life, consumers may rely on recommendations or make choices based on limited information. For example, when choosing a smartphone, a consumer might base their decision on a friend's recommendation rather than a detailed comparison of specifications.
5. **Overemphasis on Utility**:
   - *Critique*: Utility is not the sole driver of consumer decisions. Psychological factors such as emotions, habits, and perceptions of fairness can influence choices. For example, a consumer may donate to charity for moral satisfaction, even if there is no tangible utility gain.
6. **Ignores Constraints Beyond Budget**:
   - *Critique*: While the budget constraint is central to Consumer Choice Theory, other limitations such as time, accessibility, and cognitive effort are often significant. For example, a consumer may buy a pricier snack near the checkout because it's convenient, even if a cheaper option is available further away.
7. **Unrealistic Mathematical Modeling**:
   - *Critique*: The mathematical models used assume preferences are smooth and continuous, which is often not the case. Real-world preferences can be discontinuous and hard to quantify. This is why combining data-driven insights with qualitative research like focus groups and interviews is essential to understanding consumer behavior.
8. **Overlooks Long-Term Decision-Making**:
   - *Critique*: The theory typically emphasizes immediate utility maximization and neglects long-term considerations. For instance, a consumer might choose to invest in a gym membership despite the upfront cost for long-term benefits like improved health.
9. **Assumption of Homogeneity**:
   - *Critique*: The theory presumes uniform behavior among consumers facing similar circumstances. In reality, individual differences such as personality, upbringing, and life experiences result in varied decision-making patterns. Two consumers with the same budget may prioritize different products based on their unique values and experiences.

Wrap - Up

Utility and Consumer Choice Theory are valuable for helping you understand consumer decisions and the reasons behind them. However, it's important to remember that these are just theories and do not account for the imperfect nature of human behavior. We don't always make decisions based solely on logic; we often make them based on emotions. People can be irrational, and decisions influenced by emotions are common. Understanding this aspect can give you a better insight into why certain goods and services are purchased. Ultimately, mastering these economic concepts can help you understand:

- Consumer behavior and preferences.
- How changes in income, prices, or product features influence purchasing decisions.
- The impact of taxes, tariffs, and subsidies on consumption patterns.

Chapter 5: Perfect Competition, Monopolies, and Market Differentiation

Different Market Structures

Economics isn't just about numbers—it's about understanding the environments where businesses operate. Market structures shape everything from pricing strategies to how much power businesses have in the marketplace. In this next chapter of the book, we are going to explore different market structures and how they impact the choices that businesses make.

Learning about different market structures is arguably one of the most important concepts to understand in economics, whether you are a marketer or anyone else, because understanding these structures will also help you better grasp the policies that governments and regulators use to affect competition in the marketplace.

Being that we are all citizens of some nation, it is always wise to be knowledgeable about these concepts. The structures we are going to look at are perfect competition, monopoly, monopolistic competition, oligopoly, monopsony, oligopsony, duopoly, natural monopoly, and contestable market. Let's get started.

Perfect Competition

A market structure where many sellers and buyers trade identical products. No single player has enough influence to dictate the price, which is set purely by supply and demand.

Characteristics:

- Many small sellers and buyers.
- Products are identical or highly substitutable.
- No single seller controls the price; it's determined by supply and demand.
- Easy entry and exit from the market.

Farmers selling wheat or corn exemplify perfect competition. If you're a wheat farmer, your product is identical to others. You can't charge more than the going rate because buyers can easily get the same wheat from someone else.

In perfect competition, businesses can't rely on branding or marketing to charge premium prices. Success comes from efficiency—producing at the lowest possible cost. For marketers, this is a rare landscape because there's no room to differentiate a product.

Monopoly

A market with one seller dominating the entire industry. This business sets the price because there are no direct competitors. Barriers to entry (like patents or high startup costs) protect the monopoly from competition.

Characteristics:

- Single seller dominates the market.
- Unique product with no close substitutes.
- High barriers to entry.

Think of your local utility company providing electricity. You don't have alternatives because it's not practical for multiple companies to build competing power grids.

Monopolies control pricing and supply, but they must tread carefully to avoid backlash from regulators or customers. Marketing in a monopoly focuses on building goodwill and justifying pricing—think corporate responsibility campaigns or community sponsorships.

Monopolistic Competition

A market where many sellers offer similar but not identical products. Each business differentiates its product through branding, quality, or other features.

Characteristics:

- Many sellers offer similar but slightly differentiated products.
- Branding, quality, or features set products apart.
- Low barriers to entry.

The fast-food industry all sell burgers, but their branding and unique menu items set them apart. Also, tech companies generally make the same products, but their branding and design set them apart.

In this market structure, differentiation is key. Successful businesses in this structure emphasize branding, customer experience, and unique selling points. The more distinctive your offering, the better you compete.

Oligopoly

A market dominated by a few large players who control most of the market share. These companies often influence prices and work in tandem to maintain their dominance.

Characteristics:

- Few dominant sellers control the market.
- Products can be identical (e.g., oil) or differentiated (e.g., smartphones).
- High barriers to entry.

The airline industry is an example. Major carriers dominate the market, with smaller airlines struggling to compete. The banking industry is another example because of regulations and the way the industry is structured; it is generally harder for smaller banks to compete.

For smaller businesses, entering an oligopoly is challenging due to high barriers. Marketing strategies in an oligopoly focus on loyalty programs, partnerships, and brand trust. For big players, collaboration (and sometimes competition) with other giants shapes their strategy.

Monopsony

A market where there is only one buyer, but many sellers. This buyer wields significant power to dictate prices.

Characteristics:

- Single buyer controls the market.
- Many sellers compete to sell to the buyer.

The U.S. government purchasing military equipment is an example. Defense contractors rely on this single buyer for their sales.

If you're the seller in a monopsony, your pricing power is limited. Marketing in a monopsony focuses on meeting the unique demands of the buyer, offering superior value, and building relationships.

Oligopsony

A market where a few buyers dominate and control pricing, while many sellers compete for their business.

Characteristics:

- Few buyers control the market.
- Sellers must compete for their business.

The coffee industry is an example. Small coffee bean farmers rely on a few multinational buyers to purchase their crops. The digital advertising industry is another example, where only a few companies offer ad space and control prices.

For sellers, the key is forming strong partnerships with buyers and leveraging quality or certifications (like Fair Trade) to stand out. Marketing helps emphasize these differentiators to appeal to big buyers.

Duopoly

A market dominated by two powerful sellers. Both compete intensely but also depend on each other to some extent.

Characteristics:

- Only two sellers dominate the market.
- High barrier to entry.

The soda industry is a great example, it dominated by two main companies. The phone market is another example. Their rivalry has defined the market for decades.

In a duopoly, brand loyalty is everything. Marketing strategies focus on building emotional connections, running campaigns that highlight differences, and continuously innovating.

Natural Monopoly

A monopoly that exists due to high startup costs or unique resources, making competition impractical or impossible.

Characteristics:

- Monopoly arises due to high infrastructure costs that make competition impractical.
- High barrier to entry.=

All monopolies, in some way, are government-granted. Water supply companies are an example; it's inefficient to have multiple companies laying water pipes in the same area. Also, electric providers generally have a monopoly in their region.

Natural monopolies often face scrutiny, so marketing focuses on transparency and community engagement. Business owners should emphasize reliability and long-term value.

Contestable Market

A market where entry and exit are relatively easy, meaning any company can challenge existing players if they see an opportunity.
Characteristics:

- Few barriers to entry.
- Existing firms can face competition at any time.

The ride-sharing industry is an example, the barrier to entry is rather low. In a contestable market, flexibility and innovation are key. Marketing efforts should focus on capturing customer loyalty and building a brand that withstands new entrants.

Wrap-Up

Each market structure presents unique challenges and opportunities. For marketers, understanding these structures informs your strategies—whether it's competing in a crowded space, differentiating a product, or navigating limited competition. For business owners, this knowledge shapes pricing, product positioning, and how you approach your market.

In the ever-evolving world of business, knowing your market structure is like having a roadmap to success. So, which one does your business operate in? And how will you leverage it?

Chapter 6: Game Theory and Strategic Decision-Making

Game theory is a powerful framework for understanding strategic interactions between different players, such as competitors, firms, or consumers. It emphasizes that outcomes for any given player depend not only on their own choices but also on the choices of others. For business owners, game theory offers a valuable perspective on making optimal decisions in competitive environments marked by uncertainty and limited information.

Essentially, it helps you figure out the best choice to make, depending on what the other person might do. It's like a way of thinking ahead and planning your moves, just like in a board game or a puzzle. In real life, companies do this too, for example:

- If two dealerships are selling cars, one might think, "Should I lower my prices or keep them the same? What will the other store do?"
- If both lower their prices, customers get a deal, but the stores make less money.
- If one lowers prices and the other doesn't, the cheaper store gets more customers.

By thinking about what others might do, companies can make smarter choices. That's game theory in action.

Key Concepts in Game Theory

Understanding the core ideas of game theory, such as the Prisoner's Dilemma, Nash Equilibrium, and Payoffs, can help businesses navigate complex competitive environments.

- The **Prisoner's Dilemma** illustrates a situation where two individuals must decide whether to cooperate or act in their own self-interest, without knowing what the other will do. Cooperation produces the best collective result, but fear of betrayal often drives both parties to act selfishly, leading to suboptimal outcomes for everyone.
- This scenario ties directly to the concept of **Nash Equilibrium**, where each player's strategy is the best response to the other's, even if it doesn't lead to the most optimal outcome overall. For example, in the Prisoner's Dilemma, both players blaming each other is a Nash Equilibrium because neither has an incentive to unilaterally change their strategy.
- **Payoffs** in game theory represent the rewards or losses each player receives based on their choices and those of others. These concepts help explain why businesses sometimes prioritize self-interest even when cooperation could produce better outcomes for all.

Game Theory in Competitive Advertising

In advertising, game theory provides insights into how businesses can optimize their strategies. Imagine two companies competing in the same market, each deciding how much to spend on advertising. If both heavily advertise, they may increase their market share but at a significant cost. If only one invests heavily, that company gains an edge at a lower relative cost. Conversely, if neither invests, both save money but risk losing potential growth.

Game theory helps predict the likely balance in such scenarios, where businesses often settle on a middle ground—spending enough to remain competitive without overspending in an advertising war. This balanced approach often occurs in industries with intense competition, where companies must navigate between maximizing visibility and minimizing unnecessary expenditures.

Pricing Strategies and Market Competition

Game theory also applies to pricing decisions, particularly in industries prone to price wars. When one company lowers prices to attract customers, competitors may follow suit, leading to reduced profit margins across the board. Anticipating such moves allows businesses to strategize whether to match price cuts, differentiate their offerings, or focus on customer value instead.

In industries dominated by a few players, like airlines or telecommunications, companies frequently base their pricing strategies on competitors' potential responses. The goal is to optimize outcomes without triggering destructive pricing battles. Game theory encourages businesses to consider the broader implications of their pricing decisions and how those choices affect their competitive positioning.

Anticipating Competitor Actions

One of the most valuable applications of game theory is the ability to anticipate competitors' responses. When planning a product launch, for instance, a business can analyze how competitors might react—whether by introducing a competing product, lowering prices, or emphasizing unique features. By predicting these responses, businesses can adjust their strategies, such as timing the launch strategically or introducing promotions that competitors will find hard to replicate.

Similarly, game theory is useful in deterring new entrants to a market. Established businesses might lower prices, increase advertising, or strengthen customer loyalty to make market entry less appealing for competitors. On the other hand, cooperation between competitors

—such as aligning on industry standards or refraining from mutually destructive price wars—can also be a strategic outcome.

Wrap Up

Game theory is a framework for understanding strategic interactions between different players (competitors, firms, consumers, etc.) where the outcome for each player depends not only on their own choices but also on the choices of others. For business owners and marketers, game theory offers insights into how businesses can make optimal decisions when facing competition, limited information, and uncertainty.

By analyzing the strategic moves of competitors, companies can decide whether to react aggressively (e.g., cutting prices, launching counter-campaigns) or innovatively (e.g., improving customer service or introducing unique features). Game theory shows that cooperation can sometimes be the optimal strategy—like when companies in a market agree not to engage in cutthroat pricing wars or agree to cooperate on a standard (think of mobile phone companies agreeing on charging ports to reduce consumer frustration).

Key Takeaways

- Game theory is crucial for anticipating and responding to competitor moves. Business owners and marketers can leverage game theory to predict competitive behavior and make more informed decisions about pricing, advertising, and product positioning.
- Competitive strategies like pricing wars and advertising campaigns can be understood as games. By using game theory models, business owners and marketers can make decisions that optimize their outcomes and avoid losing ground to competitors.
- Strategic interactions are never one-sided. The decisions of others impact a company's strategy, and using game theory, marketers can plan their next moves based on what others are likely to do.

By framing game theory within the context of business decision making—like pricing, advertising, and product launches—you are able to see how economic theory directly influences real-world decision making strategies, and how economists have used game theory to predict behaviors of consumers, businesses, and policy makers.

Chapter 7: Behavioral Economics and Consumer Psychology

Understanding the psychology behind how consumers make decisions is a critical step in mastering products and services are effectively sold. Behavioral economics merges psychology and economics, revealing that humans are not always rational beings who weigh pros and cons in a spreadsheet-like manner.

Instead, our decisions are often influenced by biases, emotions, and cognitive shortcuts. While I hinted at this concept in **Chapter 3: Price Elasticity of Demand and Consumer Behavior**, this chapter will dive deep into the topic.

Key Concepts of Behavioral Economics

For business owners and marketers, understanding these concepts is like having a roadmap to influence consumer behavior in subtle yet powerful ways. By leveraging these principles, campaigns can feel intuitive, persuasive, and deeply impactful.

Here are the concepts that we will discuss: **Loss Aversion, Anchoring, Status Quo Bias, Endowment Effect, Hyperbolic Discounting, Choice Overload, Social Proof, Availability Heuristic, Framing Effect, Prospect Theory, Mental Accounting, Sunk Cost Fallacy, Default Bias, Reciprocity, Priming, Confirmation Bias, Time Inconsistency, Loss Framing, Herd Behavior, Overconfidence Bias, Decoy Effect.**

Loss Aversion

People experience the pain of losing something more intensely than the joy of gaining something of equal value. Streaming services that offer free trials capitalize on this principle—once consumers experience the benefits, they often hesitate to cancel, fearing the "loss" of those perks.

Anchoring

The first piece of information a person encounters heavily influences their decision-making. For example, a car dealership might list an original price of $30,000 before offering the vehicle for $25,000. The higher initial price serves as an anchor, making the discount appear more significant.

Status Quo Bias

People tend to stick with what they know, resisting change even when better options are available. Many consumers remain loyal to their default internet provider or bank simply because switching feels too much like an effort.

Endowment Effect

Ownership increases perceived value. Sellers on platforms like eBay often overprice items because they attach more value to their possessions than buyers do.

Hyperbolic Discounting

Immediate rewards are more appealing than future benefits, even when the latter is more advantageous. People might choose to binge-watch a series today rather than work on a project due next week, prioritizing instant gratification over long-term goals.

Choice Overload

Too many options can overwhelm consumers, leading to indecision. A grocery store displaying 30 types of jam is less likely to see purchases than one offering only six varieties.

Social Proof

People look to the actions of others to guide their own, especially in uncertain situations. A crowded restaurant signals quality, attracting even more patrons compared to an empty one next door.

Availability Heuristic

Decisions are influenced by how easily examples come to mind. After hearing about a plane crash on the news, some people overestimate the risks of flying, despite it being one of the safest modes of travel.

Framing Effect

How information is presented can shape decision-making. A yogurt labeled "90% fat-free" is more appealing than one labeled "10% fat," even though both are identical.

Prospect Theory

People evaluate potential gains and losses relative to a reference point rather than in absolute terms. A $20 discount on a $100 product feels more significant than the same discount on a $1,000 item.

Mental Accounting

People mentally categorize money, affecting how they use it. For instance, a $50 gift card might feel more indulgent than $50 in cash, even though they have the same purchasing power.

Sunk Cost Fallacy

Individuals continue investing in something because of the time, money, or effort already spent, even when it's no longer beneficial. Finishing a boring movie simply because you've watched half of it is a common example.

Default Bias

Pre-set options often dictate choices. Many employees stick with their employer's default retirement savings plan instead of exploring custom options, simply because it's easier.

Reciprocity

People feel compelled to return favors. Offering free samples in stores often increases the likelihood of a purchase, as recipients feel a sense of obligation.

Priming

Subtle cues can influence behavior unconsciously. For example, playing French music in a wine shop can boost sales of French wine by subtly steering customers' choices.

Confirmation Bias

People interpret information in ways that confirm their existing beliefs. A consumer loyal to a brand may focus on positive reviews while ignoring negative feedback.

Time Inconsistency

Decisions often favor the present self over the future self. For example, indulging in fast food today while planning to start a diet tomorrow highlights this inconsistency.

Loss Framing

Highlighting what someone might lose by not acting can be more persuasive than emphasizing potential gains. A fitness ad stating, "Don't miss your chance to lose those extra pounds" is often more compelling than one that promises, "Gain the body you've always wanted."

Herd Behavior

People follow the crowd, assuming the group's decision is the correct one. Long lines outside Apple stores for product launches create buzz and encourage others to join.

Overconfidence Bias

Individuals often overestimate their abilities or judgment. Entrepreneurs, for instance, may believe their startup will succeed despite the high failure rates in their industry.

Decoy Effect

Introducing a less attractive option can make another option seem more appealing. Subscription services often use this strategy by adding a third, slightly better plan to make the mid-tier option appear as the best value.

How Behavioral Insights Shape Marketing Messages and Sales Tactics

Behavioral economics is behind many persuasive sales and marketing strategies. By understanding how consumers think, businesses can craft messages that resonate on a deeper psychological level.

Framing Effects

Example: A gym advertises memberships as "Just $1 a day" instead of "$365 per year." The smaller daily amount feels more manageable, even though it's the same price.

Why It Tends to Work: Framing costs in relatable terms reduces the perceived barrier to entry, encouraging action.

Defaults and Choice Architecture

Example: Ever notice how the "Recommended Plan" on subscription websites is pre-selected? That's choice architecture at work, nudging customers toward the most profitable option for the business.

Why It Tends to Work: Defaults exploit inertia—people often stick with pre-set choices because it's easier than making a decision.

Fear of Missing Out (FOMO)

Example: Flash sales or "Order within the next hour for same-day shipping" messages capitalize on the fear of missing out.

Why It Tends to Work: FOMO triggers loss aversion, pushing consumers toward impulsive decisions to avoid regret.

Anchoring for Discounts

Example: Displaying "Was $99, Now $49" creates the impression of a deal, even if the original price was inflated.

Why It Tends to Work: The higher anchor price makes the discount feel substantial, even if $49 was the intended price all along.

Wrap Up

Behavioral economics bridges the gap between rational theories of decision-making and the often emotional, impulsive reality of human behavior. By understanding the principles that influence how people think, feel, and act, business owners and marketers can create strategies that resonate on a deeper psychological level. It's not about manipulating customers but about meeting them where they are—acknowledging their biases, simplifying their choices, and aligning with their natural inclinations.

When applied thoughtfully, behavioral economics creates win-win scenarios where consumers feel understood, and businesses build lasting connections. At its heart, it's a reminder that understanding the "why" behind human behavior is the key to driving meaningful and impactful results.

Chapter 8: Economic Cycles and Marketing Response

I hope you are enjoying the book so far, as you can see having a detailed understanding of economics is not just about being able to save money, but more so about being able to plan ahead and anticipate the moves of businesses and policy makers, and thus be in a position to take advantage of any opportunities that arise.

In this next chapter, we are going to discuss economic cycles and how they affect business owners and consumer behavior alike.

Different Economic Cycles

Economic cycles, or business cycles, describe the recurring patterns of growth and decline in an economy over time. These cycles consist of four stages: expansion, peak, contraction, and trough.

Expansion Phase

During the **Expansion phase**, the economy experiences growth, often measured by an increase in GDP, or Gross Domestic Product, which is the total value of all goods and services produced in a country. **Consumer confidence**, which reflects how optimistic people feel about the economy, rises, leading to increased spending and investment.Businesses expand, hire more workers, and increase production.

Unemployment, the percentage of people actively seeking but unable to find work, is typically very low in this phase. For example, after the 2008 financial crisis, global economies entered a period of recovery and expansion as they rebuilt from the downturn.

Peak Phase

The **Peak** represents the height of economic activity when the economy is operating at or near full capacity. Growth begins to slow, and **Inflation**—the general rise in prices of goods and services—often accelerates due to strong demand. Wages, or earnings, typically rise during this phase as businesses compete for labor. However, this period may also see speculative investments and overconfidence.

The **dot-com bubble** of the late 1990s is an example. During this time, many internet-based companies, despite having weak or nonexistent business models, attracted enormous investments. When it became clear these businesses couldn't sustain profits, the bubble burst in

2000, leading to a sharp decline in stock prices, business closures, and an economic downturn. This where the Contraction phase comes.

Contraction Phase

Following the peak is the **Contraction phase**, also known as a **Recession**. A recession is a significant decline in economic activity lasting for at least several months, characterized by falling GDP, reduced consumer spending, and rising unemployment. The **2008 financial crisis**, for instance, was caused primarily by the collapse of the U.S. housing market. During the early 2000s, banks issued risky mortgages to borrowers with poor credit histories.

These mortgages were bundled into financial instruments called mortgage-backed securities, and synthetic collateralized debt obligations, which are extremely complex financial products that are difficult to value. Both of these products were sold to investors as a way for banking institutions to make money without having to keep a large amount of capital or liquidity on hand.

Unfortunately, when many homeowners defaulted on their loans, these securities plummeted in value, triggering a crisis in the financial sector. The resulting credit crunch made borrowing difficult, leading to reduced consumer spending, business closures, and widespread job losses worldwide.

In extreme cases, an economy may experience a **Depression**, which is a far more severe and prolonged contraction. The **Great Depression** of the 1930s is the most well-known example. It was triggered by a combination of factors, including a stock market crash in 1929, which wiped out massive amounts of wealth and shattered consumer and business confidence.

Additionally, widespread bank failures caused by poor lending practices led to the loss of savings for many Americans, further reducing spending. The resulting economic collapse led to a 25% unemployment rate in the United States and a global downturn that lasted nearly a decade.

Stagflation

Occasionally, during or after a contraction, economies experience **stagflation**, an unusual scenario where high inflation coincides with high unemployment and stagnant growth.

Stagflation is challenging to address because measures to reduce inflation, such as raising interest rates, can worsen unemployment, while policies to reduce unemployment, such as increased government spending, can fuel inflation. A notable example occurred during the 1970s oil crisis, when surging oil prices caused production costs to rise, slowing economic growth while inflation remained high.

Trough

The lowest point in the cycle is the **trough**, where economic activity bottoms out. During this phase, consumer and business confidence is at its weakest, and unemployment remains high. However, the trough is also the starting point for recovery, as businesses and consumers slowly regain confidence, setting the stage for another expansion.

Kondratiev Waves

Economic cycles can vary greatly in length and intensity. Some cycles last only a few months, while others, like the Great Depression, persist for years. Longer cycles, such as **Kondratiev waves**, which span 50–60 years, are often driven by major technological innovations or structural economic shifts. The Industrial Revolution from (1780s–1840s) is a prime example of a Kondratiev Wave that fueled the long-term cycle of economic growth during the 19th century.

These cycles are shaped by factors like **Monetary policy** (how central banks manage the supply of money and interest rates), **Fiscal policy** (government decisions on spending and taxation), geopolitical events, and technological advancements. By understanding economic cycles and their causes, policymakers, businesses, and individuals can better navigate challenges and seize opportunities for growth.

Adjusting business strategies in different economic climates

Adjusting to economic cycles is crucial for business owners and marketers to ensure resilience during downturns and capitalize on opportunities during growth periods. Each phase of the economic cycle presents unique challenges and opportunities, requiring tailored strategies.

---

1. Expansion Phase

During expansion, the economy grows, consumer confidence is high, and demand for goods and services increases. Businesses thrive as revenue and profits rise.

Strategies for Business Owners:

- **Invest in Growth:** Expand operations, hire additional staff, and invest in marketing and new products. Use the increased cash flow to scale your business.
- **Build Reserves:** While growth is exciting, save a portion of profits to prepare for potential downturns.
- **Strengthen Customer Relationships:** Build loyalty through excellent service and engagement to retain customers during future slowdowns.
- **Innovate:** Invest in research and development (R&D) to stay ahead of competitors and diversify offerings.

---

2. Peak Phase

At the peak, the economy reaches its highest point, but growth slows, and inflation often increases. Overconfidence can lead to excessive spending or speculative risks.

Strategies for Business Owners:

- **Avoid Overextending:** Resist the urge to take on excessive debt or expand too aggressively.
- **Monitor Costs:** Inflation can drive up expenses, so negotiate with suppliers and streamline operations to maintain margins.
- **Diversify Revenue Streams:** Introduce complementary products or services to protect against market shifts.
- **Prepare for Contraction:** Begin planning for a slowdown by reviewing budgets, cutting unnecessary expenses, and securing financial flexibility.

---

3. Contraction Phase (Recession)

In this phase, economic activity declines, consumer spending drops, and unemployment rises. Businesses may face reduced demand and tighter cash flow.

Strategies for Business Owners:

- **Cut Non-Essential Costs:** Focus on critical operations and delay non-urgent investments.
- **Protect Cash Flow:** Maintain a healthy cash reserve to cover operating costs and avoid risky financial commitments.

- **Focus on Core Customers:** Double down on your most loyal and profitable customers, offering promotions or loyalty rewards to maintain relationships.
- **Adapt Offerings:** Offer more affordable alternatives or essential products that are in demand during tough times.
- **Collaborate:** Negotiate better terms with suppliers and landlords to reduce expenses.

---

4. Trough Phase

The trough is the lowest point of the economic cycle. Consumer and business confidence is weak, but the economy may show early signs of recovery.

Strategies for Business Owners:

- **Position for Recovery:** Use the downtime to assess your business model, refine operations, and innovate for the upcoming expansion.
- **Invest Wisely:** If your finances allow, acquire undervalued assets, invest in training, or upgrade equipment to prepare for the next growth phase.
- **Communicate Optimism:** Reassure employees and customers that your business is stable and ready to grow as conditions improve.

Special Considerations for Unusual Cycles

Stagflation (High Inflation + Low Growth):

- **Focus on Efficiency:** Reduce waste and improve productivity to offset rising costs.
- **Price Strategically:** Avoid drastic price increases but find ways to maintain profitability through bundling or value-added services.
- **Stay Flexible:** Be ready to adapt quickly as the economy stabilizes or declines further.

Depression (Severe and Prolonged Downturn):

- **Emphasize Essentials:** Focus on providing products or services that remain in demand, even during tough times.
- **Diversify Markets:** Explore new customer segments or geographical markets less affected by the downturn.

- **Leverage Community Support:** Participate in local initiatives to build goodwill and attract customers.

Wrap Up

By understanding the characteristics of each economic cycle and proactively adjusting strategies, business owners, marketers, and every day consumers can navigate economic fluctuations effectively. The key is balancing risk management with seizing opportunities, ensuring your decision making remains resilient and positioned for long-term success.

Chapter 9: Inflation, Pricing, and Cost Management

Inflation is one of those economic forces that seems to sneak up and affect everyone, from the smallest business owner to the largest corporations—and, of course, the everyday consumer. It makes goods and services cost more over time while the same amount of money buys less. But why does inflation happen, and who—or what—is behind it?

For business owners, understanding inflation is crucial. Knowing its causes, how it impacts pricing and purchasing behavior, and strategies to navigate it can help ensure your business thrives even during challenging economic periods. Let's explore these concepts step by step.

What Is Inflation and Why Does It Happen?

At its core, inflation refers to the rise in prices across an economy over time, which reduces the purchasing power of money. For example, if inflation is 5% annually, what cost $100 last year will cost $105 this year. This doesn't happen randomly—there are underlying reasons inflation occurs.

Causes of Inflation

1. **Demand-Pull Inflation**
   Demand-pull inflation happens when demand for goods and services outpaces supply. This often occurs during economic booms when consumers and businesses have more disposable income to spend, leading to increased demand. For example, if a popular product is in limited supply but everyone wants it, sellers may raise prices.
2. **Cost-Push Inflation**
   Cost-push inflation occurs when the cost of production rises, and businesses pass these higher costs onto consumers. This can happen when raw materials, labor, or transportation costs increase. For example, if the price of oil rises, shipping and manufacturing become more expensive, driving up the prices of goods.
3. **Built-In Inflation**
   This occurs when businesses and workers anticipate future inflation and act accordingly. For instance, workers demand higher wages to keep up with rising costs, and businesses then increase prices to offset these higher wages. This creates a self-reinforcing cycle.
4. **Monetary Policy and Excess Money Supply**
   Central banks, like the Federal Reserve in the U.S., play a significant role in inflation.

When they increase the money supply—whether by printing more money or lowering interest rates—people and businesses have more to spend. While this stimulates the economy, it can also lead to demand-pull inflation if too much money chases too few goods.

Who's "Causing" Inflation?

It's tempting to blame a single group for inflation, but the reality is more complex. Here's a breakdown of key players:

- **Central Banks and Governments**: They manage monetary policy, which can directly impact inflation. For example, during economic downturns, governments often stimulate the economy by increasing spending or cutting taxes. Central banks might lower interest rates to encourage borrowing. These actions can unintentionally lead to inflation if the economy overheats.
- **Supply Chain Disruptions**: Global events, such as pandemics or conflicts, can cause supply shortages and drive up prices. When raw materials or goods become harder to obtain, businesses are forced to pay more, passing those costs to consumers.
- **Businesses and Wages**: Companies raising wages to attract and retain workers can increase production costs. While higher wages benefit employees, businesses might offset these costs by increasing prices.
- **Consumers**: Yes, even consumers contribute! When people rush to buy goods in anticipation of higher prices, they increase demand, which can exacerbate inflation.

It's a dynamic interplay of factors, and no single group is entirely to blame. Inflation reflects the collective behaviors of economies, markets, and individuals.

The Impact of Inflation on Pricing and Consumer Purchasing Power

For business owners, inflation creates a tough balancing act. Rising costs for materials, labor, and operations force you to consider price increases. Meanwhile, your customers—grappling with higher costs for food, housing, and fuel—might be less willing to spend.

When inflation rises, purchasing power declines. A family that could afford frequent dining out last year may now cook at home more often. For your business, this might mean fewer sales, smaller orders, or customers opting for cheaper alternatives.

The challenge lies in maintaining profitability while keeping customers loyal. Raising prices too much or too quickly risks driving customers away. But absorbing higher costs without adjusting prices can hurt your bottom line.

Strategies for Pricing Adjustments in Inflationary Times

Inflation forces business owners to rethink their pricing strategies. Here are ways to navigate this delicate terrain without alienating customers:

Gradual and Transparent Price Increases

Customers are less likely to resist small, incremental price increases than sudden, dramatic ones. For example, instead of a bakery increasing bread prices by $2 overnight, it might raise prices by $0.50 every few months. Transparency is key: explaining that the increase reflects rising ingredient costs can foster understanding and trust.

Reinforce Value Instead of Price Alone

Rather than focusing solely on price, emphasize the value your business offers. Highlight what sets your products apart—be it quality, sustainability, or exceptional customer service. Customers are often willing to pay a little more if they feel they're getting more in return.

Avoid Shrinkflation

Shrinkflation, where companies reduce product sizes but keep prices the same, might seem like an easy way to manage costs. However, it often backfires. Customers notice when portions shrink or packaging changes, and many have criticized businesses for being deceptive. This loss of trust can be far more damaging than a straightforward price increase.

Flexible and Tiered Pricing

Offering a range of pricing options can help retain customers during inflationary periods. For instance, a business could introduce budget-friendly options alongside premium offerings. This allows price-sensitive customers to stay engaged with your brand while maintaining higher-margin products for others.

Practical Tips for Managing Costs in High-Inflation Periods

Inflation isn't just about pricing—it's also about how you manage costs. Here's how to stay lean and efficient:

Negotiate with Suppliers

Don't accept rising supplier costs as inevitable. Reach out to negotiate better terms, explore bulk purchasing options, or find alternative vendors. Building strong relationships with suppliers can lead to cost-saving opportunities.

Streamline Operations

Look for inefficiencies in your operations. Can you reduce waste, automate tasks, or optimize workflows? Even small changes, like consolidating deliveries or switching to energy-efficient equipment, can add up.

Reassess Non-Essential Spending

Take a hard look at discretionary expenses. Do you really need that extra software subscription or the premium office supplies? Cut back where possible to free up resources for essentials.

Focus on Retention

It's more cost-effective to keep existing customers than to acquire new ones. Offer loyalty programs, personalized deals, or exclusive promotions to strengthen relationships with your current customer base.

Wrap Up

While inflation can feel like an uphill battle, it's also an opportunity to demonstrate your business's resilience and commitment to customers. By staying strategic, transparent, and value-driven, you can navigate inflation while preserving trust and loyalty.

Inflation may not be entirely avoidable, but how you respond can set your business apart. Plan thoughtfully, communicate openly, and focus on delivering value—your customers will remember how you handled the tough times.

Chapter 10: Global Economics and International Markets:

Understanding global economics is like piecing together a complex puzzle with massive rewards. For business owners, expanding into international markets means navigating challenges like exchange rates, tariffs, free trade agreements, and the unique economic landscapes of different regions. Let's unpack these concepts, explore their implications, and examine how to thrive in a global economy while considering their controversies and complexities.

The Role of Exchange Rates: How Currency Fluctuations Impact Business

Exchange rates determine the value of one currency compared to another and are pivotal for international businesses. These rates fluctuate due to factors like economic growth, interest rates, inflation, and geopolitical events. For business owners selling products or services in multiple countries, these shifts can significantly impact pricing and profitability.

Imagine you're a U.S.-based business owner selling goods in Europe. If the exchange rate changes from 1 USD = 0.9 EUR to 1 USD = 1.1 EUR, (this is just an example, not the actual rate) your products become more expensive for European buyers, potentially reducing demand unless you adjust your pricing.

On the other hand, if the exchange rate swings the other way, making your products cheaper abroad, you might see a surge in demand. However, this requires vigilance, as these changes could also squeeze your profit margins when converting sales back to your local currency. Savvy business owners keep a close eye on exchange rate trends and use tools like hedging (financial contracts to lock in favorable rates) to minimize risks and maximize stability.

Tariffs: The Hidden Costs and Controversies of International Trade

Tariffs are taxes or duties imposed on imported goods, often used to protect local industries from foreign competition. While they can benefit domestic producers by making imported goods more expensive, they also create significant challenges for businesses reliant on global trade.

For instance, a business exporting goods to a country with high tariffs might find their products less competitive compared to local alternatives. To adapt, the business owner could explore local sourcing or negotiate trade agreements to mitigate the impact of tariffs.

However, tariffs are deeply controversial. From one viewpoint, tariffs are seen as a way to protect local industries and jobs. By making imported goods more expensive, tariffs can encourage consumers to buy locally-produced items, giving domestic businesses an edge. For governments, this can mean safeguarding industries that are vital for national security or economic stability.

For instance, if a country relies heavily on imported steel but imposes tariffs on foreign steel, local producers might benefit as their goods become more competitively priced. This could preserve jobs in the steel industry and bolster the domestic economy.

However, the same tariffs that protect local industries can also backfire by increasing costs for businesses and consumers. For businesses that rely on imported materials or components, higher tariffs mean higher production costs. These costs are often passed on to consumers through increased prices, which can reduce demand and hurt the broader economy.

Take a business owner who manufactures electronics. If tariffs are placed on imported microchips, the production cost of each device rises. To stay profitable, the business might have to raise prices, potentially driving away budget-conscious customers. In this way, tariffs can ripple through the economy, affecting industries far removed from the original target of the tax.

At the heart of the controversy is the fact that tariffs create clear winners and losers. While some industries benefit from reduced competition, others suffer from higher costs and limited market access. For consumers, the overall impact depends on whether they gain from a stronger local economy or lose out because of higher prices for goods.

Free Trade: Not Always the Golden Solution

While free trade agreements aim to reduce barriers like tariffs and promote the unrestricted exchange of goods and services between countries, they're not always as beneficial as they seem. The North American Free Trade Agreement (NAFTA), for example, eliminated many tariffs between the U.S., Canada, and Mexico, but its effects have been hotly debated.

Supporters argue that NAFTA boosted trade and economic growth across North America. Critics, however, highlight that it led to the outsourcing of manufacturing jobs from higher-wage countries to lower-wage ones, creating economic imbalances. Small businesses in sectors like agriculture also faced increased competition, which sometimes drove local producers out of business.

This illustrates that while free trade can lower costs and expand markets, it also has downsides, particularly for industries unable to compete with cheaper imports. For business owners, understanding these dynamics is crucial when navigating international markets.

Navigating International Markets with an Economic Perspective

Entering international markets involves more than just shipping products overseas. It requires a comprehensive understanding of the economic conditions and cultural nuances of each region.

Start by assessing a country's economic stability. Factors like inflation, unemployment, and consumer spending patterns can provide insights into potential challenges and opportunities. For instance, in a country with high inflation (the general rise in prices over time), consumer purchasing power may shrink. Adapting by offering smaller, more affordable product sizes can help maintain demand without overwhelming buyers.

Cultural differences also play a significant role. In some regions, consumers may value savings over spending, impacting how luxury or premium products perform. In others, rapid economic growth might fuel trends like conspicuous consumption, where people prioritize displaying their wealth. Aligning your product offerings and marketing strategies with these cultural and economic priorities can make or break your success in a new market.

Legal and regulatory frameworks also need consideration. Trade agreements, environmental regulations, and labor laws vary widely between countries and can significantly impact your operations. For instance, countries with strict environmental policies might require changes to packaging or production methods, while others with relaxed trade barriers might offer cost-saving opportunities.

Real-World Examples: Adapting to Economic Environments

Consider a business owner expanding into a region with high tariffs on imported goods. To remain competitive, the business might set up a local manufacturing facility. This not only avoids tariffs but also builds goodwill by supporting the local economy through job creation.

In another case, a business entering a country with volatile exchange rates might hedge its currency risks. By locking in favorable exchange rates or pricing products in the local currency, the business can minimize financial uncertainty and protect its profit margins.

Lastly, imagine entering a region where inflation is rampant. To address the reduction in consumer purchasing power, the business could adjust its offerings to focus on smaller, more affordable options or explore bundling strategies that provide better value for money.

Wrap - Up

Global economics is the backdrop to every business decision in international markets. Exchange rates, tariffs, and free trade agreements are not just abstract concepts but tangible forces shaping the opportunities and risks of global trade.

While exchange rates require vigilance and strategy, tariffs and free trade agreements demand a nuanced understanding of their benefits and drawbacks. By staying informed, adapting to local conditions, and anticipating economic trends, business owners can navigate these complexities and position themselves for sustainable growth in the dynamic world of international markets.

Chapter 11: Budgeting and Investing: The Economics of ROI

Every person should know that managing money effectively is key to success, but understanding how to get the most bang for your buck—economically speaking—is where the magic happens. This section dives deep into budgeting and investing from an economic perspective, focusing on *Return on Investment (ROI)* and marginal analysis. We'll explore how to allocate budgets smartly and discuss tools for measuring and optimizing your economic impact. It's primarily written for business owners, but it can honestly apply to anyone! Let's get started.

What Is ROI, and Why Does It Matter?

ROI, or *Return on Investment*, is a simple but powerful concept. It measures how much profit or value you gain relative to the money you spend. Think of it like planting a garden: if you invest in seeds, water, and fertilizer, you'll want the garden to produce enough vegetables to justify the effort and cost. If your garden gives you more food than the cost of planting it, you've achieved a positive ROI.

Mathematically, ROI is calculated as:

$$ROI = \frac{Net\ Profit}{Investment\ Cost} X\ 100$$

For example, if you spend $1,000 on marketing and generate $4,000 in sales, your net profit is $3,000 ($4,000 - $1,000). The ROI would be:

$$ROI = \frac{3{,}000}{1{,}000} X\ 100 = \ 300\%$$

This means you've made three times the amount you spent. Business owners use ROI to evaluate whether their spending decisions are worthwhile.

The Role of Marginal Analysis: The Fine Line of Spending Wisely

Marginal analysis is another essential concept for smart budgeting. It helps you determine whether spending a little more will lead to enough additional benefit to make it worthwhile.

Here's a real-world example: imagine you own a bakery and have a $500 monthly budget for social media ads. After spending $500, you've gained 50 new customers. Now, you're considering spending an extra $100. Marginal analysis asks: will that additional $100 bring in enough extra customers to make it worth spending?

If that extra $100 only brings in five more customers, the return per customer might not justify the added expense. But if those five customers are big spenders or loyal customers who will keep coming back, the additional investment could pay off over time.

Marginal analysis encourages business owners to weigh costs and benefits carefully. You don't just throw money at problems—you think critically about whether each dollar spent brings meaningful returns.

How to Allocate Budgets Based on Economic Value

Allocating your budget is a balancing act. It's not just about spending on what's popular or trendy but about directing money toward activities or strategies that provide the highest ROI.

Step 1: Prioritize High-Impact Activities

Start by identifying areas of your business that consistently deliver results. For example, if email campaigns regularly bring in loyal customers, consider allocating more money there rather than experimenting with a platform that hasn't proven effective yet.

Step 2: Consider the Law of Diminishing Returns

This is an economic principle that states that at a certain point, adding more resources (money, time, effort) won't yield proportionally higher benefits. For example, doubling your budget for social media ads might not double your sales. Once you reach an optimal level of spending, returns start to level off or even decline.

Knowing when to stop increasing spending in one area allows you to redirect funds to other parts of your business that might yield higher returns.

Step 3: Experiment, but Measure Results

Experimentation is essential to growth, but it should be done cautiously. Allocate a small percentage of your budget for testing new strategies, tools, or platforms. Track the results carefully to see if they perform better than existing methods. If something works, shift more funds in that direction; if not, move on.

Tools for Measuring and Optimizing Economic Impact

Today's business world offers an abundance of tools that make ROI tracking and optimization easier. Let's discuss some categories of tools and how they can help:

Analytics Platforms

These tools track where your money is going and how much value it's creating. For example, analytics software can show which advertising campaigns bring in the most traffic, sales, or leads. This data helps you decide where to invest more and where to cut back.

Financial Dashboards

Dashboards let you visualize your spending and ROI across different areas of your business. They consolidate key data points like income, expenses, and profits, giving you a clear overview of how your business is performing.

A/B Testing Software

A/B testing involves comparing two versions of a strategy to see which performs better. For example, if you're running ads, you might test two headlines to see which gets more clicks. Over time, these small tweaks can significantly improve ROI.

Budget Allocation Models

Some tools use algorithms to help you decide where to allocate your budget for maximum impact. These tools often use historical data to predict where your money will be most effective, saving you the guesswork.

Wrap - Up

By thinking like an economist and acting like a savvy business owner, you can make smarter choices with your budget. Remember, every dollar spent is an investment in your business's future, and understanding the economics of ROI ensures those investments deliver the results you need.

To maximize ROI and optimize your economic impact:

1. Understand how ROI works and use it as a guide for spending decisions.
2. Use marginal analysis to evaluate whether additional investments are worthwhile.
3. Allocate your budget to high-impact areas while experimenting cautiously.
4. Leverage tools and technology to track performance and make data-driven decisions.

Chapter 12: Data, Forecasting, and Market Trends

CPI (Consumer Price Index) and PCE (Personal Consumption Expenditures): Tracking the Cost of Living

The **Consumer Price Index (CPI)** measures the average change in prices that consumers pay for a basket of goods and services over time. Think of CPI as a "cost of living tracker" that reflects how prices fluctuate for everyday items like groceries, housing, and transportation.

CPI is often used to gauge inflation—when prices rise across the board, reducing purchasing power. For business owners, a rising CPI might mean higher operational costs and more price-sensitive customers. You could respond by offering discounts, emphasizing value, or finding ways to cut production costs.

However, CPI has its critics. It doesn't account for all spending categories (such as investment assets), and its methodology can distort actual inflation rates. For example, CPI measures the cost of a fixed basket of goods, which doesn't always reflect how people adjust their purchasing habits over time.

Interestingly, the **Federal Reserve**—the central bank responsible for monetary policy in the United States—prefers different inflation measures: the **Personal Consumption Expenditures (PCE) Price Index** and **Core Personal Consumption Expenditures (Core PCE) Price Index**, which excludes food and energy price fluctuations. PCE is considered more comprehensive because it accounts for changes in consumer behavior, such as substituting cheaper alternatives when prices rise. Core PCE is an even more comprehensive inflation measure because it excludes food and energy from the CPI, as these goods tends to fluctuate more dramatically in pricing than other goods.

GDP (Gross Domestic Product): The Economy's Scorecard

GDP measures the total value of all goods and services produced within a country. It's often used to assess whether an economy is growing or contracting. A healthy, growing GDP suggests strong economic activity and consumer confidence, which might encourage you to invest in expansion, new products, or hiring.

However, GDP is far from flawless. Over time, the methodology for calculating GDP has changed, incorporating adjustments for inflation, technological progress, and even illegal activities like black-market transactions (in some countries). These changes can make it difficult to compare GDP figures across decades or between countries. **Real GDP** may be a better measure of economic growth because it accounts for inflation, i.e excess government spending and taxation.

Moreover, GDP doesn't always reflect the full picture. For example, it excludes unpaid work like caregiving and overlooks income inequality. Also modern GDP numbers do not take into account government spending on social programs, immigration, or subsidies. So because of this the number itself can be overly influenced by excess government spending. A rising GDP might make the economy look strong, but reality it might not be sustainable, or give a real picture of what the economy is really like.

Unemployment Rates: The Labor Market's Pulse

Unemployment rates measure the percentage of people in the workforce who are jobless but actively seeking work. A low unemployment rate often indicates a healthy economy, with more people earning and spending. For business owners, this could mean opportunities to sell higher-end products or services.

On the flip side, high unemployment may signal economic challenges, with customers focusing on essentials rather than luxuries. In such cases, you might shift your strategy to emphasize affordability or introduce financing options.

However, the way unemployment is calculated has also changed over time. Modern unemployment rates underreport joblessness by excluding discouraged workers (those who've stopped looking for work) or people working part-time who want full-time jobs. Also it only takes into account individuals who have only been unemployed for a short time, not those who have been unemployed for a long time.

This inconsistency makes it important to pair unemployment data with other metrics, such as labor force participation rates, to get a clearer picture of economic conditions.

Making Data-Driven Business Decisions Using Economic Insights

Economic indicators are valuable, but they're most powerful when combined with your business's unique data. Let's make this practical:

Imagine you own a clothing boutique. If CPI is rising, you know inflation is making everything more expensive for your customers. You might adjust by stocking more affordable items, running promotions, or focusing on durable, high-value pieces that justify the price.

Also by looking at PCE, you might consider creating more cheaper/affordable alternatives to your original products, to capture more of the market.

Now, suppose GDP is showing steady growth. This could signal a strong economy, where customers are more willing to splurge. You might decide to introduce premium products or invest in a marketing campaign to attract higher-end customers. B

But if GDP slows and unemployment rises, it's time to pivot. You might reduce inventory of luxury items, focus on staples, and double down on customer retention efforts.

Economic data can also help with timing. For example, if forecasts suggest a strong holiday season, you can ramp up advertising and inventory to meet demand. If a slowdown is expected, you can tighten budgets and focus on maintaining steady sales.

These are just scenario, being that these metrics unfortunately can be easily manipulated and misused, you should use the multiple data scores and actually conversation from your customer base to make your final decisions.

Wrap -Up

Economic data provides a wealth of insights, but it's not a magic wand. By understanding indicators like CPI, PCE, GDP, and unemployment rates—and recognizing their limitations—you can make informed, strategic decisions for your business.

Remember, no single metric tells the full story. Combining economic insights with your internal data, customer feedback, and industry trends will help you navigate uncertainty and seize opportunities. The goal isn't to predict the future perfectly but to adapt intelligently to whatever the market throws your way.

Conclusion

As we conclude this exploration of economics through the lens of modern business, it's time to reflect on the key principles we've covered and how they can empower you to run a more strategic and resilient business. By embracing an economic mindset, you'll be better equipped to navigate challenges, seize opportunities, and create a thriving enterprise. Let's break down these takeaways in a way that's practical, relatable, and actionable for you as a business owner.

Revisiting Key Economic Principles for Success

Running a business, or making consumer decisions without a grasp of fundamental economic principles is like sailing without a compass. Throughout this book, we've covered essential topics that form the foundation of an economic mindset. Here's a quick recap:

- **Supply and Demand Dynamics**: Understanding how prices and availability affect consumer behavior and market equilibrium.
- **Price Elasticity**: Learning how sensitive your customers are to changes in pricing and how it impacts your revenue.
- **Utility** and **Consumer Choice Theory**: Understanding how consumers make decisions based on the value they perceive in a product or service.
- **Market Structures**: Differentiating between perfect competition, monopolies, oligopolies, and other market types to tailor your strategies effectively.
- **Game Theory**: Anticipating competitors' moves and making informed strategic decisions.
- **Behavioral Economics**: Leveraging insights into consumer psychology to shape your business and marketing strategies.
- **Economic Cycles**: How to describe the recurring patterns of growth and decline in an economy over time, and how to use them to predicate consumer behavior These cycles consist of four stages: expansion, peak, contraction, and trough.
- **Inflation and Cost Management**: Adapting pricing and budgeting in response to fluctuating economic conditions.
- **Opportunity Cost**: Recognizing the trade-offs of every decision you make, from investments to resource allocation.
- **Budgeting** and **Investing:** How to calculate ROI (return on Investment) and use that knowledge to guide your company.

- **Data Forecasting:** How to use metrics like CPI (consumer price index), PCE (personal consumption expenditures), GDP (gross domestic product), and Unemployment rate to predict consumption and revenue.

These principles are not all theoretical—they're tools you can use to make smarter, more confident decisions in every aspect of your business.

Building Resilience Through Economic Awareness

Every person faces challenges that test their ability to adapt and persevere. By thinking like an economist, you can respond to these challenges with greater clarity and strategy.

Take inflation as an example. When prices rise across the board, it impacts both your costs and your customers' ability to spend. An economic mindset allows you to adjust pricing, negotiate better terms with suppliers, or reframe your offerings to highlight value and affordability. For instance, during inflationary periods, offering discounts on bundled services or emphasizing long-term savings from your products can help maintain customer loyalty without compromising profitability.

Understanding market cycles is equally critical. Economic awareness lets you anticipate changes in consumer behavior, prepare for seasonal shifts, and respond proactively to market disruptions. For example, if you know your industry tends to slow down in the winter, you can use that time to plan new initiatives, streamline operations, or invest in marketing campaigns for the busier months ahead.

Economic knowledge also builds confidence in decision-making. Imagine a competitor lowering their prices. Instead of panicking, you can evaluate whether this move is sustainable for them. You might recognize that maintaining your unique value proposition, rather than engaging in a price war, is a smarter long-term strategy.

For Business Owners: Economic Insight Can Help

When you understand economic principles, you elevate yourself beyond being just a business owner—you become a strategist and visionary.

For instance, understanding consumer behavior allows you to make better decisions about how to position your products and services. Behavioral economics teaches us that people often act irrationally, influenced by emotions and biases. Loss aversion, for example, shows that customers are more motivated to avoid losing something than to gain something new. Framing an offer as "Avoid missing out on this exclusive deal!" can be far more effective than simply promoting a product's features.

An economic mindset also helps you focus on long-term growth rather than short-term wins. Instead of only chasing immediate sales, you can think about building customer lifetime value—the total revenue a customer generates over their relationship with your business. By prioritizing quality, loyalty programs, and excellent service, you create a foundation for sustained success.

Finally, economics helps you adapt to changing circumstances. Whether it's identifying opportunities in a shifting market or making tough decisions during a downturn, your ability to think strategically and analyze trends will set you apart.

Final Thoughts

Adopting an economic mindset is one of the most powerful tools in your arsenal. It empowers you to see the bigger picture, think critically about your decisions, and adapt to the ever-changing landscape of the modern economy.

This doesn't mean you need a degree in economics. Instead, it's about applying key principles in practical ways—anticipating challenges, leveraging opportunities, and making decisions rooted in logic and strategy.

As you move forward, remember that every consumer decision has an economic foundation, whether it's comparing different products and services, hiring a team (for businesses), or allocating budgets and expenses. By embracing the insights you've gained, you can position yourself as a resilient and forward-thinking leader.

So keep asking the right questions, stay curious, and approach every challenge with the confidence of someone who understands the forces shaping the market. Because with the right mindset, you're not just living at the mercy of the economy—you're becoming a valuable member of it! Take care!

About the Author

Roggie Clark, also known as Raj Clark, is a 9-year SEO (Search Engine Optimization) Marketing agency owner and well published author on the subjects of SEO, HTML, CSS, Javascript, and Economics.

Raj has worked extensively with a wide range of clients in the United States, from eCommerce, B2B (Business to Business), Healthcare, enterprise companies and marketing agencies.

He is regarded as an expert, and guru by his colleagues, and the SEO industry. Raj currently lives in Maryland with his sister and niece.

www.ingramcontent.com/pod-product-compliance
Lightning Source LLC
LaVergne TN
LVHW080000210926
848481LV00012B/3630
* 9 7 9 8 2 9 5 4 6 7 9 0 5 *